IOANNIS VASILEIOU

TAXATION AND FRAUD PREVENTION IN THE EUROPEAN UNION

*LESSONS LEARNED
AND FUTURE PROSPECTS*

ATHENS 2019

ART DIRECTOR: SOFIA LIVIERATOU, sofialiv@hotmail.com

ACKNOWLEDGEMENTS
To my beloved Maria Nikou
for her encouragement and moral support

TABLE OF CONTENTS

INTRODUCTION .... Page 6

CHAPTER 1: TAXATION AND THE EUROPEAN UNION: IS IT FAIR ENOUGH? .... Page 13

CHAPTER 2: THE EUROPEAN ANTI-FRAUD POLICY: OLAF'S TREMENDOUS SIGNIFICANCE AND MULTIFARIOUS ROLE .... Page 32

CHAPTER 3: CONCLUDING REMARKS .... Page 60

BIBLIOGRAPHY .... Page 63

INTRODUCTION

The issues of taxation and fraud prevention are of pivotal significance for the entire European Union (EU) particularly these days. We must not forget that the Union is still trying to recover from perhaps its most devastating economic crisis of all times (Bettendorf et al., 2010; Devereux and Loretz, 2012; European Anti-Fraud Office, 2019; European Commission/Taxation, 2015 and 2018; European Union, 2019; European Union/Taxation, 2018; Janeba and Peters, 1999; Lierse, 2012; Radaelli, 1995; Vasileiou, 2013a, 2014a, 2017b, 2017c, 2018b, 2018c, 2019a and 2019b).

We can incontrovertibly argue that more than a few member states have successfully overcome most of the crisis' consequences but some others, such as Greece, are still being severely tortured and the future does not seem much optimistic at least in our opinion (Bettendorf et al., 2010; Devereux and Loretz, 2012; European Anti-Fraud Office, 2019; European Commission/Taxation, 2015 and 2018; European Union, 2019; European Union/Taxation, 2018; Janeba and Peters, 1999; Lierse, 2012; Radaelli, 1995; Vasileiou, 2013a, 2014a, 2017b, 2017c, 2018b, 2018c, 2019a and 2019b).

Nonetheless, despite the economic situation of individual member states, a fairer tax system accompanied by a highly successful fraud prevention mechanism are pivotal factors towards growth and prosperity, which may eventually lead to a higher degree of social stability (Bettendorf et al., 2010; Devereux and Loretz, 2012; European Commission/Taxation, 2015 and 2018; European Union, 2019; European Union/Taxation, 2018; Janeba and Peters, 1999; Radaelli, 1995).

Taxation and fraud prevention are incontrovertibly linked and, as we will see in the following chapters, they play a key role within the entire EU framework due to the fact that they actually determine a wide range of policies (European Anti-Fraud Office, 2019; European Commission/Taxation, 2015 and 2018; European Union, 2019; European Union/Taxation, 2018; Janeba and Peters, 1999; Radaelli, 1995).

In the context of this book our dominant objective is the methodical provision of a number of useful guidelines in a systematic and simplified way, in order for the reader to become familiar with the particular noteworthiness of numerous elements that characterize both the Union's taxation policy and its incessant fight against corruption (European Anti-Fraud Office, 2019; European Commission/Taxation, 2015 and 2018; European Union, 2019; European Union/Taxation, 2018; Janeba and Peters, 1999; Vasileiou, 2013a, 2014a, 2017b, 2017c, 2018b, 2018c, 2019a and 2019b).

According to EU official data of 2018, the European Parliament has concluded that €50-70 bn are actually lost to tax fraud, evasion and avoidance annually and this is an exceedingly high amount (European Anti-Fraud Office, 2019; European

Commission/Taxation, 2015 and 2018; European Union, 2019; European Union/Taxation, 2018; Vasileiou, 2013a, 2014a, 2017b, 2017c, 2018b, 2018c, 2019a and 2019b).

It is not difficult to understand that taxation is an outstandingly critical component due to the fact that, inter alia, offers citizens access to healthcare, public infrastructure and education of high quality (European Commission/Taxation, 2015 and 2018; European Union, 2019; European Union/Taxation, 2018; Vasileiou, 2013a, 2014a, 2017b, 2017c, 2018b, 2018c, 2019a and 2019b).

Apart from that, the momentousness of fair taxation lies in the fact that it can offer priceless assistance towards the creation of a much-needed "safety net" for the more vulnerable (European Commission/Taxation, 2015 and 2018; European Union, 2019; European Union/Taxation, 2018).

This factor deserves particular attention as it is directly linked with the aforementioned argument about the reduction of socioeconomic disparities which, despite the Union's several systematic attempts, still exist (European Commission/Taxation, 2015 and 2018; European Union, 2019; European Union/Taxation, 2018).

What is more, we must not forget that fair taxation can incontrovertibly contribute towards maintaining a competitive and sustainable economy as well as a top-class business environment (European Commission/Taxation, 2015 and 2018; European Union, 2019; European Union/Taxation, 2018).

It would not be an exaggeration to argue that tax evasion and avoidance gradually erode national revenues and this can indubitably result in a significant decrease of the available funds for public spending and investment. Such a phenomenon irrefutably calls for immediate action due to the fact that its consequences might be devastating (European Commission/Taxation, 2015 and 2018; European Union, 2019; European Union/Taxation, 2018).

We must also add that tax abuse in reality undermines the social contract between citizens and their governments and this is a huge moral issue. In the context of several cases, governments indeed compensate for the revenue losses by taxing workers, citizens and small businesses more (European Commission/ Taxation, 2015 and 2018; European Union, 2019; European Union/Taxation, 2018).

In practice, this action clearly undermines the fundamental principle of fair burden sharing. This detail deserves particular attention and it is not difficult to understand why (European Commission/Taxation, 2015 and 2018; European Union, 2019; European Union/Taxation, 2018).

It goes without saying that the Union budget efficaciously finances numerous projects and programs. Therefore, it is only natural that a) any improper use of EU budget funds and b) any evasion of taxes, duties and levies that fund the Union budget results in a significant damage to EU citizens (European Anti-Fraud Office, 2019; OLAF/What we do, 2019; Vasileiou, 2013a, 2014a, 2017b, 2017c, 2018b, 2018c, 2019a and 2019b).

In order to combat all these extremely harmful effects, the European Anti-Fraud Office (Office de Lutte Anti-Fraude-OLAF) is the sole Union body mandated to investigate, detect and stop fraud with Union funds (European Anti-Fraud Office, 2019; OLAF/What we do, 2019; Vasileiou, 2013a, 2014a, 2017b, 2017c, 2018b, 2018c, 2019a and 2019b).

As we repeatedly mention in this book, the entire EU anti-fraud mechanism is closely related to tax issues and, hence, examining tax matters in parallel with fraud findings can incontrovertibly lead us to more than a few interesting conclusions (European Anti-Fraud Office, 2019; OLAF/What we do, 2019; Vasileiou, 2013a, 2014a, 2017b, 2017c, 2018b, 2018c, 2019a and 2019b).

Apart from the introduction, this book comprises three chapters. In Chapter 1, titled *"Taxation and the European Union: Is it Fair Enough?"* we attempt to methodically elucidate the most notable components in terms of taxation in the Union.

Of course we do not imply that tax policies are not fair and such a detail must be made crystal clear. What we mean is that tax policies can possibly become fairer in order for the citizens' precise needs and objectives to be addressed in a more satisfactory manner.

Therefore, we attempt a scrupulous examination of the exact way according to which the relevant Union policies take place and critically focus on a number of significant elements, such as the Common Consolidated Corporate Tax Base (CCCTB), the Digital Single Market, the Digital Services Tax, and the three pillars on which the Union's Agenda for the much-needed fair taxation is based.

In Chapter 2, named *"The European Anti-Fraud Policy: OLAF's Tremendous Significance and Multifarious Role"*, the entire spectrum of EU activities in order to successfully combat fraud is being critically presented.

It is true that the abovementioned spectrum is extremely complex and multidimensional, but we remain certain that the specific method of analysis on which we have relied simplifies everything.

As expected, special emphasis is placed on the particularly noteworthy role and tasks of OLAF, the rigorous examination of which remains our pivotal concern. Concomitantly, miscellaneous significant factors, namely the "Hercule Programmes", the Irregularity Management System (IMS) and the Early Detection and Exclusion System (EDES) are being meticulously scrutinized towards a deeper understanding.

Finally, in Chapter 3, the foremost *"Concluding Remarks"* are being systematically drawn, in order for the principal points to be efficaciously summarized. It is not difficult to realize that less corruption results in a higher degree of growth, development and social stability.

And of course in such cases, a far more suitable tax system in favor of the common interest can irrefutably become a reality. In the following chapters we attempt to shed light on a number of interesting and perhaps unknown facts that can indeed determine the Union's future economic prosperity and can lead to a more functional integration, always with a view to the desirable yet increasingly difficult target of socioeconomic cohesion.

CHAPTER 1

TAXATION AND THE EUROPEAN UNION: IS IT FAIR ENOUGH?

In the context of this chapter, we methodically focus on a number of key points that relate to the particularly crucial sector of taxation in the Union in a direct or indirect way. Following our hitherto conducted research, we draw the conclusion that in general tax evasion and avoidance can unquestionably become a foremost threat in the context of both the economic and sociopolitical sector in all member states without a single exception (Bettendorf et al., 2010; Devereux and Loretz, 2012; European Commission/Taxation, 2015 and 2018; European Union, 2019; European Union/Taxation, 2018; Janeba and Peters, 1999; Lierse, 2012; Radaelli, 1995; Vasileiou, 2013a, 2014a, 2017b, 2017c, 2018b, 2018c, 2019a and 2019b).

We believe that a functional taxation policy accompanied by a rapid elimination of illegal economic practices can indeed contribute to the coveted reduction of both economic and social disparities within the entire Union. And it is only natural that such a reduction can result in a deeper and more functional integration, which has always been a pivotal EU objective

(Bettendorf et al., 2010; European Anti-Fraud Office, 2019; European Commission/Taxation, 2015 and 2018; European Union, 2019; European Union/Taxation, 2018; Janeba and Peters, 1999; Lierse, 2012; Radaelli, 1995).

The first issue that needs to be clarified is that the EU does not actually play a direct role in either setting tax rates or raising taxes (Bettendorf et al., 2010; Devereux and Loretz, 2012; European Commission/Taxation, 2015 and 2018; European Union, 2019; European Union/Taxation, 2018; Janeba and Peters, 1999; Lierse, 2012).

Taxes are in fact decided by member states, while the Union is actually in charge of methodically overseeing the (tremendously critical) wider framework of national tax rules so as to efficaciously guarantee that that they are indeed consistent with specific Union policies which attempt to a) satisfactorily safeguard the free movement of capital, goods and services in the single market, b) systematically encourage and promote both job creation and economic development, which are components of paramount significance especially these days, c) methodically ensure that taxes do not lead to any discrimination at all against workers, consumers or businesses from other member states and d) efficaciously guarantee that businesses in one country are not characterized by an unfair advantage over competitors in another (European Union, 2019; European Union/Taxation, 2018; Lierse, 2012; Vasileiou, 2013a, 2014a, 2017b, 2017c, 2018b, 2018c, 2019a and 2019b).

It is worth noting that the decisions of the Union on tax matters require unanimity by all member governments and this is a detail which must under no circumstances go unnoticed (European Commission/Taxation, 2015 and 2018; European Union, 2019; European Union/Taxation, 2018).

In our opinion, this unanimity in practice protects the interests of all member states, as their voice is being seriously taken into consideration. This element reveals once more the unity that exists between member states and can incontrovertibly be characterized as an encouraging step towards the desirable (and surely much-needed) deeper integration (European Commission/Taxation, 2015 and 2018; European Union, 2019; European Union/Taxation, 2018).

In terms of certain taxes, such as the Value Added Tax (VAT) or taxes on petrol, tobacco and alcohol (excise duties), all member states have actually reached an agreement towards aligning their rules and minimum rates. The target of this decision is to manage to avoid the distortion of competition across borders within the Union (European Union, 2019; European Union/Taxation, 2018; Keen et al., 1996; Vasileiou, 2013a, 2014a, 2017b, 2017c, 2018b, 2018c, 2019a and 2019b).

As far as company and income tax are concerned, the Union's foremost target is to methodically guarantee the full respect for the fundamental principles of non-discrimination and free movement in the context of the single market (European Union, 2019; European Union/Taxation, 2018; Keen et al.,

1996; Vasileiou, 2013a, 2014a, 2017b, 2017c, 2018b, 2018c, 2019a and 2019b).

In order for the abovementioned target to eventually become a reality, a specifically coordinated Union approach is absolutely essential among member states. What is more, we believe that such an approach will be incontrovertibly useful in order for miscellaneous burning issues (like tax evasion) to be adequately addressed (European Union, 2019; European Union/Taxation, 2018; Keen et al., 1996).

Apart from that, it is a common assumption that tax avoidance seriously disrupts fair competition between businesses within the particularly neuralgic single market framework. Should we wish to be more precise, we argue that numerous smaller or local companies actually suffer tremendously serious competitive distortions simply because of the "aggressive" tax practices of their larger competitors (European Commission/Taxation, 2015 and 2018; European Union, 2019; European Union/Taxation, 2018; Vasileiou, 2013a, 2014a, 2017b, 2017c, 2018b, 2018c, 2019a and 2019b).

Incontrovertibly, this element totally contradicts the EU general philosophy and principles and must be efficaciously addressed as soon as possible in order for further tribulations that may threaten the Union's economic stability to be avoided (European Commission/Taxation, 2015 and 2018; European Union, 2019; European Union/Taxation, 2018; Vasileiou, 2013a, 2014a, 2017b, 2017c, 2018b, 2018c, 2019a and 2019b).

Another important issue is tax revenue and we have to point out that the Union has no say in terms of the way countries spend their tax revenues. Nonetheless, it is important to emphasize the fact that the Union's economies are highly interdependent. This means that countries which overspend and go into an extremely high amount of debt will probably create numerous increasingly thorny problems within the already fragile eurozone (European Union, 2019; European Union/Taxation, 2018; Vasileiou, 2013a, 2014a, 2017b, 2017c, 2018b, 2018c, 2019a and 2019b).

We are all familiar with the potential consequences of such a malfunctioning and, hence, we can detect more than a few systematic attempts by member states in order to manage to sufficiently coordinate their economic policies (European Union, 2019; European Union/Taxation, 2018; Vasileiou, 2013a, 2014a, 2017b, 2017c, 2018b, 2018c, 2019a and 2019b).

This coordination partly relies on a number of highly noteworthy recommendations by the Commission. Moreover, it is essential to note that quite a few of these recommendations indeed refer to national tax policies (European Union, 2019; European Union/Taxation, 2018; Vasileiou, 2013a, 2014a, 2017b, 2017c, 2018b, 2018c, 2019a and 2019b).

As far as personal and company taxes are concerned, it is important to stress that they are mainly the responsibility of individual member states. Nevertheless, according to Union rules, they must not hinder mobility in Europe (European Union, 2019; European Union/Taxation, 2018).

Additionally, we have to stress that companies investing across borders or individuals moving to another member state can either come across incredibly complex administration, or face taxation in two or more countries (European Union, 2019; European Union/Taxation, 2018).

It is true that more than a few treaties towards the adequate elimination of double taxation exist between most member states. Nonetheless, they may fail to sufficiently cover all taxes or the entire context of cross-border situations. Apart from that, they might not to be able to efficaciously apply in practice. These problems are indubitably serious both for the present and the future. Hence, the Commission has been ceaselessly attempting to come up with adequate resolutions (European Union, 2019; European Union/Taxation, 2018).

We also have to mention that some of the Union's measures include, inter alia, a) taking legal action in cases of discrimination or breaking of EU law whenever necessary and b) methodically proposing certain coordinated solutions to governments (European Union, 2019; European Union/Taxation, 2018; Vasileiou, 2013a, 2014a, 2017b, 2017c, 2018b, 2018c, 2019a and 2019b).

The particular momentousness and usefulness of the single market is a given, therefore member states have successfully reached important agreements in order to sufficiently range their rules for taxing services and goods (European Union, 2019; European Union/Taxation, 2018; Vasileiou, 2013a, 2014a, 2017b, 2017c, 2018b, 2018c, 2019a and 2019b).

This way, competitive distortions among businesses will probably be avoided and of course businesses will be much more benefited by the single market which permits free trade in terms of services and goods. Following a meticulous scrutiny of numerous EU documents, we argue that minimum tax rates are in place for VAT and excise duties, along with specific rules on the method according to which these taxes must be applied (European Union, 2019; European Union/Taxation, 2018; Keen et al., 1996).

What is more, governments are indeed free to apply their own national rates above the Union's minimums. The Union's VAT system is irrefutably functional, but the Commission is ceaselessly conducting numerous attempts to make it less complicated and perhaps a bit more efficacious as far as the revenues it delivers to national governments are concerned (European Union, 2019; European Union/Taxation, 2018; Keen et al., 1996).

One of the dominant concerns in the context of the taxation system is for tax laws of one country not to offer people the opportunity to escape taxation in another. Such a feature would result into countless serious tribulations. A rapid and systematic EU-wide action is more than urgent should we take into account the cross-border nature of tax evasion and avoidance (European Union, 2019; European Union/Taxation, 2018).

So far we can only praise the numerous decisive EU steps towards that direction and we must highlight the fact that currently the Union indeed has an action plan and more than a few attention-grabbing initiatives either in place or under development (European Union, 2019; European Union/Taxation, 2018; Vasileiou, 2013a, 2014a, 2017b, 2017c, 2018b, 2018c, 2019a and 2019b).

These initiatives include, among other things, a) a fast and methodical reaction mechanism to battle VAT fraud and b) specific important rules on information exchange between member states. We must also underline that the Union systematically focuses on fair company taxation, which is one of its principal priorities within the always multidimensional taxation spectrum (European Union, 2019; European Union/Taxation, 2018; Keen et al., 1996).

Regrettably, certain companies practice an "aggressive tax planning" towards minimizing their tax bills based on loopholes between tax systems of different countries. We actually believe that a constructive and well-performed coordination accompanied by a highly satisfactory information sharing between tax administrations can indeed eliminate such unacceptable phenomena that indubitably result in an outstandingly negative impact (European Union, 2019; European Union/Taxation, 2018; Vasileiou, 2013a, 2014a, 2017b, 2017c, 2018b, 2018c, 2019a and 2019b).

Furthermore, the Union's governments must be capable of guaranteeing that their corporate tax regimes a) do not unfairly entice firms away from other member states or otherwise destroy the tax base there and b) are indeed fair and open. We are aware that, to this end, they have actually signed up to a code of conduct promising to avoid acting in that manner (European Union, 2019; European Union/Taxation, 2018; Vasileiou, 2013a, 2014a, 2017b, 2017c, 2018b, 2018c, 2019a and 2019b).

At this point, it is essential to further elucidate the pivotal CCCTB, which is rightly regarded as a cornerstone towards an innovative fair corporate tax system. The latter can actually offer adequate assistance in order for the single market to significantly flourish both in the near and the distant future (Bettendorf et al., 2010; European Commission/Taxation, 2015 and 2018; European Union, 2019; European Union/Taxation, 2018).

The CCCTB was initially proposed in 2011 and was relaunched in an enhanced version five years later. Based on our research, we can conclude that it can be characterized as the exact model of a fair corporate tax system, which will probably lead to a high degree of growth and progress (Bettendorf et al., 2010; European Commission/Taxation, 2015 and 2018; European Union, 2019; European Union/Taxation, 2018).

One of its foremost advantages is that it will sufficiently facilitate doing business in the Union mainly due to the fact that there would be solely one rulebook for companies to effectively calculate their taxable profits throughout the Union, as well as a "one-stop-shop" system to file tax returns (Bettendorf et al., 2010; European Commission/Taxation, 2015 and 2018; European Union, 2019; European Union/Taxation, 2018).

According to the Union, companies could be in position to offset losses in one part of Europe against profits in another. Such a procedure will take place in the same way as at national level and this element deserves particular attention (Bettendorf et al., 2010; European Commission/Taxation, 2015 and 2018; European Union, 2019; European Union/Taxation, 2018).

Special emphasis must be placed on the fact that the CCCTB actually provides companies that invest in growth-friendly activities with tax incentives. Concurrently, another principal CCCTB objective is to offer satisfactory assistance in order for tax avoidance to be substantially cut out (Bettendorf et al., 2010; European Commission/Taxation, 2015 and 2018; European Union, 2019; European Union/Taxation, 2018).

Additionally, we have to point out that the largest multinationals would all be adequately covered by the CCCTB system, while the foremost channels of tax avoidance would be methodically removed (Bettendorf et al., 2010; European Commission/Taxation, 2015 and 2018; European Union, 2019; European Union/Taxation, 2018).

Apart from that, we must not ignore the fact that the CCCTB's highly systematic anti-abuse measures would provide significant help in order to rapidly stop companies from shifting profits out of the single market. This is another interesting detail that can serve as food for thought in terms of numerous important issues

(Bettendorf et al., 2010; European Commission/Taxation, 2015 and 2018; European Union, 2019; European Union/Taxation, 2018).

Based on our research, the CCCTB could in reality raise investment in the Union by up to 3.4%, while EU businesses could reduce their compliance costs by 2.5%. Furthermore, according to official EU data of 2018, the CCCTB is currently being negotiated by member states which have to agree on it unanimously (Bettendorf et al., 2010; European Commission/Taxation, 2015 and 2018; European Union, 2019; European Union/Taxation, 2018).

The Digital Single Market is another crucial component that must be seriously taken into account due to the fact that it must incontrovertibly rely on an effective taxation system. It is true that nowadays corporate tax rules are slightly insufficient in order to substantially cover digital companies (European Commission/Taxation, 2015 and 2018; European Union, 2019; European Union/Taxation, 2018; Vasileiou, 2013a, 2014a, 2017b, 2017c, 2018b, 2018c, 2019a and 2019b).

Therefore, in spring 2018, the Commission proposed a number of Union resolutions towards the adequate taxation of digital economy. These resolutions included, inter alia, a basic reform of the precise method according to which companies are taxed in the context of the Single Market, in order for new business forms to be actually reflected in a more efficient manner (European Commission/Taxation, 2015 and 2018;

European Union, 2019; European Union/Taxation, 2018; Vasileiou, 2013a, 2014a, 2017b, 2017c, 2018b, 2018c, 2019a and 2019b).

Apart from that, they also included a new Digital Services Tax, which will apply to the "hardest-to-capture" digital activities, while the comprehensive reform is systematically being put in place. Based on official EU data of 2018, we can argue that the Union's Agenda for the highly desirable fair taxation is actually based on three equally noteworthy pillars. The first is "transparency", the second the "effective taxation" and the third the "global good governance" (European Commission/Taxation, 2015 and 2018; European Union, 2019; European Union/Taxation, 2018).

As far as tax transparency is concerned, in 2015, the Commission managed to successfully launch its tremendously noteworthy fair taxation campaign with a notable Tax Transparency Package (European Commission/Taxation, 2015 and 2018; European Union, 2019; European Union/Taxation, 2018).

The foremost objective is the achievement of an even higher cooperation and openness between member states within the always problematic context of tax issues (European Commission/Taxation, 2015 and 2018; European Union, 2019; European Union/Taxation, 2018).

It is not an exaggeration to mention that member states have indeed reached several agreements for an efficacious automatic information exchange on a) multinationals' country-by-country reports and b) tax rulings. These steps are incontrovertibly gigantic towards a fairer and far more functional taxation system (European Commission/Taxation, 2015 and 2018; European Union, 2019; European Union/Taxation, 2018; Vasileiou, 2013a, 2014a, 2017b, 2017c, 2018b, 2018c, 2019a and 2019b).

What is more, new Union rules are expected to guarantee that tax authorities indeed have access to anti-money laundering information and such a detail unambiguously deserves particular attention (European Commission/Taxation, 2015 and 2018; European Union, 2019; European Union/Taxation, 2018; Vasileiou, 2013a, 2014a, 2017b, 2017c, 2018b, 2018c, 2019a and 2019b).

We must not ignore the fact that member states have actually begun to methodically share specific information with regard to citizens' financial accounts abroad. We remain perfectly sure that this element eventually ends bank secrecy in the Union (European Commission/Taxation, 2015 and 2018; European Union, 2019; European Union/Taxation, 2018; Vasileiou, 2013a, 2014a, 2017b, 2017c, 2018b, 2018c, 2019a and 2019b).

Furthermore, the Commission has already proposed a) transparency requirements for intermediaries and b) public country-by-country reporting for multinationals. The target is for a higher degree of oversight of advisors' and companies' activities to be systematically provided (European Commission/

Taxation, 2015 and 2018; European Union, 2019; European Union/Taxation, 2018; Vasileiou, 2013a, 2014a, 2017b, 2017c, 2018b, 2018c, 2019a and 2019b).

Additionally, the Union has already signed Transparency Agreements with Switzerland (May 2015), Liechtenstein (October 2015), San Marino (December 2015), Andorra (February 2016) and Monaco (July 2016) (European Commission/Taxation, 2015 and 2018; European Union, 2019; European Union/Taxation, 2018).

The "effective taxation" is the second pillar and we remain perfectly sure that a dominant objective of the Union is to methodically guarantee that all companies without the slightest exception indeed pay tax where they make their profits. This assumption and the relevant procedure might seem pretty obvious and perhaps too easy, but the truth is quite different (European Commission/Taxation, 2015 and 2018; European Union, 2019; European Union/Taxation, 2018; Vasileiou, 2013a, 2014a, 2017b, 2017c, 2018b, 2018c, 2019a and 2019b).

A truly effective taxation is an extremely difficult task and therefore the Commission proposed the Anti-Tax Avoidance Directive (ATAD 1&2) under which more than a few specific and absolutely essential legally-binding anti-abuse measures are set for the entire Union. It goes without saying that this is another decisive step towards a better taxation system (European Commission/Taxation, 2015 and 2018; European Union, 2019; European Union/Taxation, 2018; Vasileiou, 2013a, 2014a, 2017b, 2017c, 2018b, 2018c, 2019a and 2019b).

The abovementioned new measures enter into force in 2019, while their fundamental pursuit is to rapidly close the most significant "paths" for tax avoidance that exist nowadays. Such an initiative will incontrovertibly result in a wide range of multidimensional benefits which will give further boost to the already heavily tortured EU economy (European Commission/Taxation, 2015 and 2018; European Union, 2019; European Union/Taxation, 2018; Lierse, 2012).

We also have to highlight the review of preferential regimes (patent boxes) and transfer pricing rules which was launched in order to successfully prevent tax avoidance via the aforesaid paths (European Commission/Taxation, 2015 and 2018; European Union, 2019; European Union/Taxation, 2018).

Apart from that, several state aid cases have indisputably challenged unfair tax benefits that a number of member states actually gave to certain multinational companies. These details must under no circumstances go unnoticed since, at least in our opinion, reveal a highly systematic, indubitably ambitious and indeed mature planning (European Commission/Taxation, 2015 and 2018; European Union, 2019; European Union/Taxation, 2018; Vasileiou, 2013a, 2014a, 2017b, 2017c, 2018b, 2018c, 2019a and 2019b).

As numerous scholars have repeatedly mentioned, the economic crisis clearly highlighted how closely connected the economies of member states are. Hence, a harmonious and methodical cooperation is more than essential. That is why they eventually reached an agreement in order to functionally coordinate their economic policies via the "European Semester" (European Commission/Taxation, 2015 and 2018; European Union, 2019; European Union/Taxation, 2018; Vasileiou, 2013a, 2014a, 2017b, 2017c, 2018b, 2018c, 2019a and 2019b).

In the context of the latter, the Commission manages to efficaciously identify both economic and social priorities for the Union and each member state for the year ahead. It is necessary to underline that, rather expectedly, within the wider framework of these publications, taxation and aggressive tax planning indeed feature highly (European Commission/Taxation, 2015 and 2018; European Union, 2019; European Union/Taxation, 2018; Vasileiou, 2013a, 2014a, 2017b, 2017c, 2018b, 2018c, 2019a and 2019b).

Another attention grabbing element is that in terms of the aforementioned context, a series of outstandingly notable suggestions and recommendations with regard to a systematic enhancement of tax systems in order to become much fairer indeed appear (European Commission/Taxation, 2015 and 2018; European Union, 2019; European Union/Taxation, 2018).

After meticulously scrutinizing numerous important EU archives and documents, we have drawn the conclusion that if a number of these suggestions are taken seriously into account the benefits will be enormous. We do not underestimate the Union's admittedly significant efforts for a more efficient tax system thus far, but we strongly believe that more improvements can irrefutably take place (European Commission/Taxation, 2015 and 2018; European Union, 2019; European Union/Taxation, 2018; Vasileiou, 2013a, 2014a, 2017b, 2017c, 2018b, 2018c, 2019a and 2019b).

The third and final pillar is the "global good governance". It goes without saying that tax evasion and avoidance do not concern solely the EU and its member states. On the contrary, they are global problems and have an increasingly serious worldwide impact (European Commission/Taxation, 2015 and 2018; European Union, 2019; European Union/Taxation, 2018; Vasileiou, 2013a, 2014a, 2017b, 2017c, 2018b, 2018c, 2019a and 2019b).

More specifically, in January 2016, the Commission managed to present a new External Strategy for Effective Taxation. We remain perfectly sure that the principal goal of that strategy is to substantially enhance and adequately reinforce cooperation with the Union's global partners as regards fair tax matters. This objective is incontrovertibly difficult but the Union remains optimistic, at least for the time being (European Commission/Taxation, 2015 and 2018; European Union, 2019; European Union/Taxation, 2018).

What is more, this strategy in fact sets out the precise method according to which the Union must cope with countries that refuse to respect international good governance standards. Such a refusal may result in numerous serious tribulations, therefore, the Union must act rapidly (European Commission/Taxation, 2015 and 2018; European Union, 2019; European Union/Taxation, 2018).

Particular emphasis must be placed on the fact that the Union's "listing process" was in reality designed in order to effectively cope with non-cooperative tax jurisdictions (European Commission/Taxation, 2015 and 2018; European Union, 2019; European Union/Taxation, 2018).

Moreover, it is worth mentioning that the first EU blacklist was indeed agreed by member states in December 2017 and was published together with a "grey" list of countries that committed themselves to enhance their tax systems, in reaction to the listing process (European Commission/Taxation, 2015 and 2018; European Union, 2019; European Union/Taxation, 2018).

We must not ignore the fact that the Union incessantly monitors the situation and managed to regularly update the blacklist in a truly successful manner. Apart from that, attention must be paid to the fact that the Union gives priority to systematically supporting developing countries within the broader context of the international campaign for fair taxation (European Commission/Taxation, 2015 and 2018; European Union, 2019; European Union/Taxation, 2018).

The principal target of the Union's "Collect More, Spend Better" strategy is to further promote and increase the Union's support to low income countries towards sufficiently tackling tax abuse and satisfactorily collecting sustainable revenues (European Commission/Taxation, 2015 and 2018; European Union, 2019; European Union/Taxation, 2018).

We believe that the abovementioned elements are of paramount significance and it would not be an exaggeration to argue that they can be regarded as absolutely pivotal factors for a more constructive tomorrow with regard to both the economic and the sociopolitical sphere (European Anti-Fraud Office, 2019; European Commission/Taxation, 2015 and 2018; European Union, 2019; European Union/Taxation, 2018; Janeba and Peters, 1999; Vasileiou, 2013a, 2014a, 2017b, 2017c, 2018b, 2018c, 2019a and 2019b).

In the next chapter, the entire spectrum of EU anti-fraud policies is being meticulously scrutinized. As we will notice, the whole range of these policies is particularly complex and multidimensional, but we hope that our analysis makes everything a bit simpler.

It goes without saying that particular emphasis has been given to OLAF, which is the primary EU "weapon" in terms of that outstandingly difficult battle. The anti-fraud mechanism is closely related not only to tax, but also to numerous other fields and sectors that determine the Union's economic growth and prosperity. Fraud elimination has always been one of the foremost EU targets and further contributes towards an even closer and indubitably more trustful relationship between the Union and its citizens.

CHAPTER 2

THE EUROPEAN ANTI-FRAUD POLICY: OLAF'S TREMENDOUS SIGNIFICANCE AND MULTIFARIOUS ROLE

The Union's anti-fraud policy is a cornerstone towards a more fruitful economic future. OLAF is responsible for providing assistance to the authorities in charge of the efficient management of EU funds, both inside and outside the Union (European Anti-Fraud Office, 2019; OLAF/Anti-fraud, 2018; Vasileiou, 2013a, 2014a, 2017b, 2017c, 2018b, 2018c, 2019a and 2019b).

The dominant objective is for these specific authorities to become aware of numerous fraud types and risks and to successfully protect the Union's financial interests by preventing fraud in the most satisfactory manner (European Anti-Fraud Office, 2019; OLAF/Anti-fraud, 2018; Vasileiou, 2013a, 2014a, 2017b, 2017c, 2018b, 2018c, 2019a and 2019b).

Following our hitherto conducted research, we can eventually draw the conclusion that the foremost objectives of the Commission's Anti-Fraud Strategy are the following three: a) to satisfactorily discourage any future case of fraud via adequate penalties, b) to methodically enhance and systematically revise fraud prevention, investigation and detection techniques and c) to sufficiently recover more funds lost because of fraud (European Anti-Fraud Office, 2019; OLAF/Anti-fraud, 2018; Vasileiou, 2013a, 2014a, 2017b, 2017c, 2018b, 2018c, 2019a and 2019b).

What is more, should we wish to satisfactorily highlight the most notable methods, we can divide them into the following three equally important subcategories: a) to systematically strengthen and further elucidate the different responsibilities of the various stakeholders, b) to efficaciously introduce anti-fraud strategies per sector in the Commission and c) to guarantee that these strategies incontrovertibly cover the entire expenditure cycle and that anti-fraud measures are indubitably cost-effective and proportionate (European Anti-Fraud Office, 2019; OLAF/Anti-fraud, 2018; Vasileiou, 2013a, 2014a, 2017b, 2017c, 2018b, 2018c, 2019a and 2019b).

OLAF is a priceless component in terms of the Union's ceaseless fight against all forms of fraud. Its task is the scrupulous investigation regarding cases of fraud against the Union's budget, which is a truly gigantic mission. OLAF attempts to discover any form of corruption or serious misconduct as far as the European institutions are concerned. Additionally, it is responsible for the successful creation and advancement of the anti-fraud policy for the European Commission (European Anti-Fraud Office, 2019; OLAF, 2017; OLAF/Fraud, 2018).

In order for the reader to become more familiar with the concept and the significance of OLAF, a brief historical overview is absolutely essential.

More specifically, in 1988, the creation of the Task Force "Anti-Fraud Coordination Unit" (UCLAF) took place as part of the Secretariat-General of the European Commission. It is worth mentioning that UCLAF worked alongside national anti-fraud departments and provided the necessary assistance and coordination in order for transnational organized fraud to be successfully addressed (European Anti-Fraud Office, 2019; OLAF/History, 2018; Vasileiou, 2013a, 2014a, 2017b, 2017c, 2018b, 2018c, 2019a and 2019b).

Five years later, UCLAF's powers were substantially increased following specific recommendations from the European Parliament (European Anti-Fraud Office, 2019; OLAF/History, 2018).

In 1999, after the events that eventually resulted in the resignation of the Santer Commission, numerous significant proposals were suggested towards the much-needed establishment of a new (and perhaps more efficient) anti-fraud body (OLAF), which would be characterized by stronger investigative powers (European Anti-Fraud Office, 2019; OLAF/History, 2018).

These proposals actually led to a) the establishment of the European Anti-Fraud Office (OLAF) with an independent investigative mandate (Decision 1999/352), b) general rules with regard to OLAF investigations (Regulation 1073/1999) and c) an agreement in terms of internal investigations within the Union institutions (European Anti-Fraud Office, 2019; OLAF/History, 2018).

As we can easily conclude, 1999 was a year of pivotal significance as regards OLAF and we argue that its gradual improvements throughout the years have clearly underlined its particular momentousness (European Anti-Fraud Office, 2019; OLAF/History, 2018).

In 2000, Franz-Herman Brüner became OLAF's founding Director-General. Four years later, the European Community managed to establish the Hercule program in order to methodically promote and enhance a wide range of actions with regard to the best possible protection of its financial interests (European Anti-Fraud Office, 2019; OLAF/History, 2018).

What is more, in 2006, a deep and perfectly planned and conducted internal reorganization of OLAF became a reality. In brief, its three principal objectives were a) the efficient strengthening in terms of its management, b) to pay more attention to OLAF's operational work and c) to adequately enhance communication within OLAF (European Anti-Fraud Office, 2019; OLAF/History, 2018).

Special emphasis must be placed on the absolutely staggering feature that in 2006, for the very first time, the number of investigations conducted by OLAF on its own account equaled the number of cases in which OLAF had been assisting the authorities of member states (European Anti-Fraud Office, 2019; OLAF/History, 2018).

Four years later, the Fraud Notification System was successfully launched by OLAF and that was a truly innovative step which permitted citizens to circulate information in terms of potential fraud and corruption online (European Anti-Fraud Office, 2019; OLAF/History, 2018).

In 2011, a new and highly noteworthy European Commission strategy was adopted towards the further enhancement as far as a) the specific conditions for fraud investigations, d) fraud detection and prevention and c) recovery and deterrence were concerned. Apart from that, Giovanni Kessler was appointed Director-General (European Anti-Fraud Office, 2019; OLAF/History, 2018; Vasileiou, 2013a, 2014a, 2017b, 2017c, 2018b, 2018c, 2019a and 2019b).

On October 1, 2013, Regulation No 883/2013 on investigations by OLAF entered into force resulting in numerous notable alterations as regards OLAF's work and its relations with miscellaneous stakeholders (European Anti-Fraud Office, 2019; OLAF/History, 2018; Vasileiou, 2013a, 2014a, 2017b, 2017c, 2018b, 2018c, 2019a and 2019b).

Particular attention must be paid to the fact that the Regulation a) requires from each member state to satisfactorily designate an Anti-Fraud Coordination Service, b) further defines the rights of persons concerned and c) practically introduces a significant annual exchange of views between OLAF and the

Union institutions (European Anti-Fraud Office, 2019; OLAF/History, 2018).

Furthermore, in the same year, the Guidelines on Investigation Procedures (GIP) were successfully issued. These are specific extremely important internal rules that staff must apply so as to efficaciously guarantee that OLAF investigations take place in the appropriate manner (European Anti-Fraud Office, 2019; OLAF/History, 2018).

Two years later, after the significant organizational restructuring by the Juncker Commission, the Directorate-General for Economic and Financial Affairs (DG ECFIN) took over from OLAF the responsibility for the euro's protection. In 2018, Ville Itälä was appointed Director-General (European Anti-Fraud Office, 2019; OLAF/History, 2018).

Should we wish to adequately summarize OLAF's dominant tasks, we divide them into the following three categories: a) a systematic investigation and detection in terms of serious misconduct by the Union's staff, b) a methodical assistance to the European Commission to sufficiently formulate and implement policies towards fraud detection and prevention and c) the rigorous investigation of corruption, fraud and various illegal actions (European Commission, 2018; European Union/Fraud, 2018; OLAF, 2018; OLAF/Fraud, 2018; Vasileiou, 2013a, 2014a, 2017b, 2017c, 2018b, 2018c, 2019a and 2019b).

Another crucial element is that investigations are highly probable to directly involve interviews and inspection of premises including outside the Union. What is more, as soon as the investigation is over, OLAF recommends action to the national governments and the Union's institutions concerned. We basically mean criminal investigations, prosecution, financial recoveries, or miscellaneous important disciplinary measures. Moreover, OLAF is in charge of meticulously monitoring the precise manner according to which these recommendations are being effectively implemented (European Commission, 2018; European Union/Fraud, 2018; OLAF, 2018; OLAF/Fraud, 2018; Vasileiou, 2013a, 2014a, 2017b, 2017c, 2018b, 2018c, 2019a and 2019b).

OLAF sufficiently accomplishes independent investigations into corruption and fraud involving Union funds in order to guarantee that all EU taxpayers' money indeed reaches specific projects that can result in growth, jobs and prosperity in Europe (European Anti-Fraud Office, 2019; OLAF/What we do, 2019; Vasileiou, 2013a, 2014a, 2017b, 2017c, 2018b, 2018c, 2019a and 2019b).

We must also take into account the fact that OLAF methodically contributes towards reinforcing the citizens' trust in the Union institutions via systematic and perfectly organized investigations, as regards any phenomena of serious misconduct by either members of EU institutions or Union's staff (European Anti-Fraud Office, 2019; OLAF/What we do, 2019; Vasileiou, 2013a, 2014a, 2017b, 2017c, 2018b, 2018c, 2019a and 2019b).

OLAF can indeed investigate issues relevant to corruption, fraud and other offences affecting the Union's financial interests concerning three principal categories. The first includes all the Union's expenditure and we mean that the spending categories are agricultural policy and rural development funds, structural funds, direct expenditure and external aid (European Anti-Fraud Office, 2019; OLAF/What we do, 2019; Vasileiou, 2013a, 2014a, 2017b, 2017c, 2018b, 2018c, 2019a and 2019b).

The second category includes suspicions with regard to serious misconduct by either members of EU institutions or Union's staff, while the third a number of areas of the Union's revenue with an emphasis on customs duties (European Anti-Fraud Office, 2019; OLAF/What we do, 2019; Vasileiou, 2013a, 2014a, 2017b, 2017c, 2018b, 2018c, 2019a and 2019b).

At this point, it is necessary to mention that OLAF receives information regarding possible irregularities and fraud from numerous sources. In the majority of cases, such information results from controls by those in charge of the management of Union funds either within the European institutions or in member states (European Anti-Fraud Office, 2019; OLAF/What we do, 2019; Vasileiou, 2013a, 2014a, 2017b, 2017c, 2018b, 2018c, 2019a and 2019b).

Particular attention must be paid to the fact that all allegations received by OLAF go through an initial assessment so as to determine if the allegation falls within the remit of the Office and meets the specific criteria in order for an investigation to be opened (European Anti-Fraud Office, 2019; OLAF/What we do, 2019; Vasileiou, 2013a, 2014a, 2017b, 2017c, 2018b, 2018c, 2019a and 2019b).

Furthermore, as soon as a case is opened, it is classified under one of three specific categories. The first concerns the "internal investigations", which are administrative ones within the Union's bodies and institutions towards the successful detection of corruption, fraud and miscellaneous illegal actions that unambiguously have a negative impact on the financial interests of the European Communities. We have to add that these clearly include serious issues related to the discharge of professional duties (European Anti-Fraud Office, 2019; OLAF/What we do, 2019).

The second category comprises the "external investigations", which are administrative ones outside the Union's bodies and institutions for the detection of fraud or other irregular conduct by legal or natural persons. It is worth mentioning that cases are classified as external investigations where OLAF provides the greatest part of the investigative input (European Anti-Fraud Office, 2019; OLAF/What we do, 2019).

Finally, the third category is about the "coordination cases", in the context of which OLAF adequately contributes to certain investigations conducted by either national authorities or other Community departments. Such a contribution becomes a reality via the methodical facilitation of both the gathering and the exchange of contacts and information (European Anti-Fraud Office, 2019; OLAF/What we do, 2019).

As far as strategic analysis is concerned, it is important to highlight that OLAF conducts analysis in order to detect either threats to the Union's reputation and finances or vulnerabilities within the context of its systems. These actions are tremendously critical and require a literally perfect coordination (European Anti-Fraud Office, 2019; OLAF/Anti-fraud, 2018).

Afterwards, OLAF proceeds to specific recommendations to Commission departments and miscellaneous bodies, which are involved in the sometimes particularly neuralgic implementation of the Union budget. We must also add that OLAF systematically issues recommendations with regard to anti-fraud measures to Commission departments, EU bodies and institutions (European Anti-Fraud Office, 2019; OLAF/Anti-fraud, 2018).

Basically, its recommendations are made a) following an investigation, b) based on analysis and c) in response to draft Commission legislative proposals. In the case that OLAF comes across any systemic problems, it rapidly alerts the Commission's internal auditors (OLAF/Anti-fraud, 2018; Vasileiou, 2013a, 2014a, 2017b, 2017c, 2018b, 2018c, 2019a and 2019b).

Some of the fields where OLAF has managed to make recommendations include a) research projects, such as plagiarism, inflated staffing costs and fraudulent use of company names in order to obtain grants, b) conflicts of interest in recruitment, c) reimbursement in terms of removal costs of Union staff and d) certain customs transit processes (OLAF/

Anti-fraud, 2018; Vasileiou, 2013a, 2014a, 2017b, 2017c, 2018b, 2018c, 2019a and 2019b).

OLAF creates important casebooks as regards anonymised cases, which underline a) work procedures potentially vulnerable to fraud that are highly probable to be used in terms of a number of Commission departments, Union institutions and bodies, b) specific techniques used by fraudsters and c) fraud indicators ("red flags") (European Anti-Fraud Office, 2019; OLAF/Anti-fraud, 2018).

Apart from that, the truly admirable work of OLAF can also be revealed from the fact that, thus far, fields and areas covered indeed include a) research projects (2010), b) structural funds (2011), c) external aid (2012) and d) OLAF internal investigations (2017) (European Anti-Fraud Office, 2019; OLAF/Anti-fraud, 2018).

Moreover, we have to point out that casebooks are made available to interested Commission departments and if relevant to other bodies, institutions and member state authorities (European Anti-Fraud Office, 2019; OLAF/Anti-fraud, 2018).

Another attention-grabbing feature is that OLAF is capable of systematically organizing specific training as regard fraud detection and prevention for both internal and external Commission auditors (OLAF/Anti-fraud, 2018; Vasileiou, 2013a, 2014a, 2017b, 2017c, 2018b, 2018c, 2019a and 2019b).

What is more, it actively contributes to highly interesting seminars with regard to fraud awareness for member states.

In addition to that, it offers basic training on analytical tools, as well as training for financial managers and officers in the particularly crucial field of risk indicators (OLAF/Anti-fraud, 2018; Vasileiou, 2013a, 2014a, 2017b, 2017c, 2018b, 2018c, 2019a and 2019b).

It goes without saying that OLAF's work has been truly admirable, since between 2010 and 2017, it has managed to a) satisfactorily issue more than 2,300 recommendations for financial, administrative, judicial and disciplinary action to be taken by the competent authorities of both the Union and the member states, b) efficaciously conclude more than 1,800 investigations and c) recommend the recovery of more than €6.6 bn to the Union's budget (European Anti-Fraud Office, 2019; OLAF, 2017; OLAF/Figures, 2018; OLAF/Fraud, 2018).

We must also add that, for 2017, OLAF's budget was €60 million. It is only natural to praise OLAF's truly multidimensional activities due to the fact that they have resulted in numerous positive results towards a more heartening economic future (European Anti-Fraud Office, 2019; OLAF, 2017; OLAF/Figures, 2018; OLAF/Fraud, 2018; Vasileiou, 2013a, 2014a, 2017b, 2017c, 2018b, 2018c, 2019a and 2019b).

More specifically, following OLAF's investigative work in general a) criminals faced prosecution before national courts, b) sums unduly spent were gradually returned to the Union's budget and c) far more efficient anti-fraud safeguards were actually put in place all over Europe (European Anti-Fraud

Office, 2019; OLAF, 2017; OLAF/Figures, 2018; OLAF/Fraud, 2018; Vasileiou, 2013a, 2014a, 2017b, 2017c, 2018b, 2018c, 2019a and 2019b).

These elements must under no circumstances go unnoticed, but instead provide the Union's entire anti-fraud mechanism with impetus for even more positive results both in the near and distant future (European Anti-Fraud Office, 2019; OLAF, 2017; OLAF/Figures, 2018; OLAF/Fraud, 2018).

In 2017, OLAF a) managed to open 215 new investigations, following 1,111 preliminary analyses conducted by OLAF experts, b) satisfactorily concluded 197 investigations, issuing 309 recommendations to the relevant EU and national authorities and c) recommended the recovery of more than €3 bn to the Union's budget and it is worth stressing that this figure actually stems from major undervaluation fraud cases successfully concluded by OLAF during that particular year (European Anti-Fraud Office, 2019; OLAF, 2017; OLAF/Figures, 2018; OLAF/Fraud, 2018).

It is important to mention that the illegal actions meticulously being investigated by OLAF include, among other things, fraudulent claims, misconduct in the context of certain public procurement procedures, customs fraud and embezzlement (European Anti-Fraud Office, 2019; European Commission, 2018; European Union/Fraud, 2018; OLAF, 2018; OLAF/Fraud, 2018).

Apart from that, it is worth noting that the "Hercule Programmes" are considered to be of primary significance since they systematically fund tremendously notable actions towards the rapid and methodical prevention and tackling of corruption, fraud and various equally harmful actions that can indeed result in serious (and occasionally insurmountable) problems for the Union's financial interests (European Anti-Fraud Office, 2019; European Commission, 2018; European Union/Fraud, 2018; OLAF, 2018; OLAF/Fraud, 2018; Vasileiou, 2013a, 2014a, 2017b, 2017c, 2018b, 2018c, 2019a and 2019b).

More specifically, these actions include a) certain research activities, b) technical and operational investigation support and c) specialized training. Emphasis must be placed on the fact that they are implemented through contracts and grants (European Anti-Fraud Office, 2019; European Commission, 2018; European Union/Fraud, 2018; OLAF, 2018; OLAF/Fraud, 2018).

In other words, we irrefutably witness an excellent planning and organization, accompanied by the typical EU will to uncompromisingly stamp out any illegal practice as soon as possible. In addition to that, national customs authorities both inside and outside the Union, often accomplish more than a few outstandingly significant joint operations not only with OLAF, but also with other Union agencies in order to combat fraud and smuggling in terms of specific high-risk areas and on identified routes (European Commission, 2018; European Union/Fraud, 2018; OLAF, 2018; OLAF/Fraud, 2018; Vasileiou, 2013a, 2014a, 2017b, 2017c, 2018b, 2018c, 2019a and 2019b).

In October 2014, in terms of an international customs operation, 130 million cigarettes and more than 1.2 million counterfeit goods were seized. It is worth mentioning that the code name of that particularly successful operation was REPLICA and actually targeted the import of numerous counterfeit goods including perfumes, cigarettes, toys, fashion accessories, bicycle and car spare parts and electric devices by sea (European Commission, 2018; European Union/Fraud, 2018; McKee and Gilmore, 2016; OLAF, 2018; OLAF/Fraud, 2018; Turner, 1995; Vasileiou, 2013a, 2014a, 2017b, 2017c, 2018b, 2018c, 2019a and 2019b).

Finally, we must add that since 2002 the counterfeiting of the euro has indeed resulted in a damage of at least half a billion. This is an extraordinary amount, taking into account the economic crisis which in a number of member states has not yet been terminated (European Commission, 2018; European Union/Fraud, 2018; OLAF, 2018; OLAF/Fraud, 2018; Vasileiou, 2013a, 2014a, 2017b, 2017c, 2018b, 2018c, 2019a and 2019b).

As expected, the Union has taken its measures and is currently managing to tackle this (truly colossal) problem via A) numerous meetings of experts from specific national agencies, towards a successful joint action, B) substantial training, which is satisfactorily funded through the noteworthy "Pericles programme" for banks, national agencies, law enforcement, judicial authorities and others involved in "fighting" euro counterfeiting not only in the Union but also outside, C) special analysis as regards counterfeit coins by the "European Technical and Scientific Centre" and D) legislation with a view to a) efficaciously guarantee certain penalties for counterfeiters under national law, b) methodically coordinate action by national authorities and c) sufficiently maintain the adequate authentication measures both for banknotes and coins (European Commission, 2018; European Union/Fraud, 2018; OLAF, 2018; OLAF/Fraud, 2018; Vasileiou, 2013a, 2014a, 2017b, 2017c, 2018b, 2018c, 2019a and 2019b).

Apart from that, particular attention must be paid to the fact that one of the foremost kinds of fraud in the Union is the systematic avoidance of excise and customs duties on cigarettes, generally by smuggling. Such a phenomenon has actually turned into a scourge that urgently needs rapid and methodical action (European Commission, 2018; European Union/Fraud, 2018; McKee and Gilmore, 2016; OLAF, 2018; OLAF/Fraud, 2018; Turner, 1995).

It is true that OLAF systematically receives relevant notifications from its partner agencies as regards any suspicious movements of cargo vessels and meticulously cross-checks national intelligence with a view to the substantial production of insights regarding smuggling methods (European Commission, 2018; European Union/Fraud, 2018; OLAF, 2018; OLAF/Fraud, 2018).

So far, these procedures have incontrovertibly been successful and emphasis must be placed on the fact that over the period

2012-14, joint OLAF operations tracking vessels with national agencies actually resulted in the seizure of a) containers holding 93 million cigarettes (evading duties worth €15 million) and b) nine ships containing approximately 215 million cigarettes (evading duties worth €43 million) (European Commission, 2018; European Union/Fraud, 2018; McKee and Gilmore, 2016; OLAF, 2018; OLAF/Fraud, 2018; Turner, 1995).

Another crucial issue is the fact that, in general, activities to methodically "battle" fraud in the Union are still hampered by certain differences in rules and practices in member states. Such a phenomenon complicates things due to the fact that it leads to dissimilar degrees of protection as far as public money is concerned (European Commission, 2018; European Union/Fraud, 2018; OLAF, 2018; OLAF/Fraud, 2018).

In order for the Union to rapidly confront these matters, it is currently debating a new Directive to protect EU financial interests through criminal law (European Commission, 2018; European Union/Fraud, 2018; OLAF, 2018; OLAF/Fraud, 2018; Vasileiou, 2013a, 2014a, 2017b, 2017c, 2018b, 2018c, 2019a and 2019b).

We have to add that this directive would actually provide the legal basis for the sufficient functioning of the proposed European Public Prosecutor's Office (EPPO), which is currently being discussed by governments of the Union (European Commission, 2018; European Union/Fraud, 2018; OLAF, 2018; OLAF/Fraud, 2018).

In the case that the EPPO is eventually created, it will be in charge of adequately enhancing both the investigation and the prosecution of offences which affect the Union's budget. This role is of paramount notability and it is not difficult to understand why (European Commission, 2018; European Union/Fraud, 2018; OLAF, 2018; OLAF/Fraud, 2018).

Following our hitherto conducted research, we are in position to argue that the principal objective is the systematic provision of EU-wide enforcement, always taking into account the enormous degree of complicatedness as regards more than a few kinds of large-scale fraud (European Anti-Fraud Office, 2019; European Commission, 2018; European Union/Fraud, 2018; OLAF, 2018; OLAF/Fraud, 2018).

It is only natural that in the majority of cases, the latter directly or indirectly involve more than one country and, therefore, unavoidably extend beyond national jurisdiction (European Commission, 2018; European Union/Fraud, 2018; OLAF, 2018; OLAF/Fraud, 2018).

Thus far, OLAF has been incontrovertibly successful in terms of numerous tremendously noteworthy cases. First and foremost, it is important to mention that an investigation actually resulted in OLAF putting an end to a complex fraud scheme through which more than €1.4 million worth of EU funds that were meant for emergency response hovercraft prototypes had indeed been misappropriated (European Anti-Fraud Office, 2019; OLAF/Success stories, 2018).

In the context of another case, OLAF managed to open an investigation after receiving specific information from a Union's delegation in an African country, alleging aberrations in the context of a procurement procedure (European Anti-Fraud Office, 2019; OLAF/Success stories, 2018).

In order to be more precise, that information was about a service contract assigned to an EU-based company in charge of the selection of experts to supervise and direct roadworks financed by the Union's budget (European Anti-Fraud Office, 2019; OLAF/Success stories, 2018).

Following numerous checks, OLAF eventually discovered that the EU-based company had indeed changed the CVs of its experts in a systematic manner so as to effectively guarantee that they would meet the specific criteria. In addition to that, OLAF concluded that controls were far from satisfactory and, apart from that, there was a significantly high turnover of experts and their competences and qualifications had not been appropriately checked (European Anti-Fraud Office, 2019; OLAF/Success stories, 2018).

The examination of miscellaneous contracts of the same European company in three more African countries resulted in the discovery of not only the same method, but also the substitution of highly qualified experts with unqualified last-minute replacements. As expected, OLAF made recommendations for the recovery of the amounts by means of financial damages and penalties of up to 10% of the contract, totally amounting to €3 million (European Anti-Fraud Office, 2019; OLAF/Success stories, 2018).

Furthermore, OLAF recommended a) the exclusion of the contractor from Union funding for a certain time, b) that databases of experienced experts in terms of projects financed by Union funds should be created and c) that obligatory financial sanctions should be definitely applied in these cases (European Anti-Fraud Office, 2019; OLAF/Success stories, 2018).

In terms of another case, OLAF received information from a specific Union institution that one of its members had been actually "filing claims" for the reimbursement of his travel expenses according to certain supporting documents that were highly probable to have been somehow falsified (European Anti-Fraud Office, 2019; OLAF/Success stories, 2018).

In 2017, another burning case systematically investigated by OLAF concerned the evasion of anti-dumping and countervailing duties imposed on solar panels sent from, or originating in China (European Anti-Fraud Office, 2019; OLAF/Success stories, 2018).

In order to become more precise, we argue that it was alleged that solar panels were incorrectly declared on importation into the Union as actually being of Taiwanese origin. Following more than a few OLAF actions, it was revealed that around 2,500 container loads of Chinese solar panels had in reality been transshipped through Taiwan to the Union (European Anti-Fraud Office, 2019; OLAF/Success stories, 2018).

According to OLAF evidence, these solar panels imported into the Union were not of Taiwanese origin as declared. Therefore, OLAF issued a financial recommendation amounting to €135 million (European Anti-Fraud Office, 2019; OLAF/Success stories, 2018).

And of course we cannot forget OLAF's methodical coordination of efforts to satisfactorily battle tobacco smuggling not only throughout the Union, but also in non-EU countries. More specifically, for numerous years OLAF had been systematically investigating suspicious actions which eventually resulted in the detection of a huge cross-Europe cigarette smuggling network (McKee and Gilmore, 2016; OLAF/Success stories, 2018; Turner, 1995).

OLAF cooperated in a highly satisfactory manner within the broader context of the criminal investigations, which were jointly organized by the relevant German and Italian authorities (European Anti-Fraud Office, 2019; OLAF/Success stories, 2018).

What is more, in autumn 2013, in terms of that procedure, OLAF managed to efficaciously organize an outstandingly noteworthy meeting involving both German and Italian law enforcement and judicial authorities and worked with Hungary, Belgium, Moldova, Ukraine, Lithuania, Romania, Slovakia and Poland (European Anti-Fraud Office, 2019; OLAF/Success stories, 2018).

We have to mention that the smuggling network actually produced cigarettes in the Union and afterwards either carried out real exports, or simulated fictional exports to non-EU countries. Afterwards, it managed to somehow smuggle the cigarettes back into the Union, therefore avoiding taxes and customs duties (European Anti-Fraud Office, 2019; OLAF/ Success stories, 2018).

Finally, the network was destroyed in November 2014 via the highly functional joint work by a) the German Zollkriminalamt Köln and Zollfahndungsamt Berlin and b) the Italian Agenzia delle Dogane and Guardia di Finanza (European Anti-Fraud Office, 2019; OLAF/Success stories, 2018).

According to EU official data of 2018, investigations are still continuing, but the important feature is that so far 10 people have been arrested. It is essential to mention that, according to the same data, the estimated damage to the Italian budget alone is more than €90 million, an amount not at all insignificant (European Anti-Fraud Office, 2019; OLAF/Success stories, 2018).

The Union clearly argues that the final figures are highly probable to be significantly higher and such a detail deserves particular attention as it unambiguously highlights the entire damage (European Anti-Fraud Office, 2019; OLAF/Success stories, 2018; Vasileiou, 2013a, 2014a, 2017b, 2017c, 2018b, 2018c, 2019a and 2019b).

OLAF's significance is no less than paramount and we strongly believe that via the meticulous scrutiny of the aforementioned cases there should be no doubt in the reader's mind. We remain perfectly sure that in the future OLAF's role will be much more important (European Anti-Fraud Office, 2019; OLAF/Success stories, 2018; Vasileiou, 2013a, 2014a, 2017b, 2017c, 2018b, 2018c, 2019a and 2019b).

The Protocol to Eliminate Illicit Trade in Tobacco Products has been a colossal step towards the effective confrontation of the nightmarish illegal tobacco trade at an international level. More specifically, the Protocol entered into force on September 25, 2018 and according to official EU data of 2018, it has 48 Parties including the Union (European Anti-Fraud Office, 2019; OLAF/Anti-fraud, 2018).

Furthermore, following the entry into force of the Protocol, the First Session of the Meeting of the Parties to the Protocol became a reality on October 8-10, 2018, in Geneva (European Anti-Fraud Office, 2019; OLAF/Anti-fraud, 2018).

In the context of that highly notable meeting, the Parties a) reached an agreement in order to create specific working groups in terms of assistance and cooperation, and on tracing and tracking the precise movement of tobacco products and b) methodically discussed the way to prioritize the work in order for the Protocol to be adequately implemented (European Anti-Fraud Office, 2019; OLAF/Anti-fraud, 2018).

It is also worth mentioning that the second Meeting of the Parties will take place in 2020 and we are indeed looking forward to become aware of the results and the future planning (European Anti-Fraud Office, 2019; OLAF/Anti-fraud, 2018;

Vasileiou, 2013a, 2014a, 2017b, 2017c, 2018b, 2018c, 2019a and 2019b).

OLAF manages to methodically gather data not only from its own operations, but also from numerous other sources, such as Court of Auditors reports, Commission audits, commercial sources, open sources (for instance public registers, the internet and press articles) and national partner authorities (European Anti-Fraud Office, 2019; OLAF/Anti-fraud, 2018; Vasileiou, 2013a, 2014a, 2017b, 2017c, 2018b, 2018c, 2019a and 2019b).

Apart from that, OLAF sufficiently shares a number of its information via the IMS. The latter contains more than a few specific details as regards fraud and irregularities in terms of the use of funds managed by the national authorities and the Commission within the context of a) structural and cohesion funds, b) agricultural policy funding and c) pre-accession funds. Moreover, we must not ignore the fact that the IMS is open to all the departments of the Commission on a need-to-know basis (European Anti-Fraud Office, 2019; OLAF/Anti-fraud, 2018; Vasileiou, 2013a, 2014a, 2017b, 2017c, 2018b, 2018c, 2019a and 2019b).

As far as the principal uses of the IMS are concerned, we would argue that they involve a) the preparation for audits, b) decisions with regard to signing off the accounts for previous operational programs and c) reporting and analysis (European Anti-Fraud Office, 2019; OLAF/Anti-fraud, 2018; Vasileiou, 2013a, 2014a, 2017b, 2017c, 2018b, 2018c, 2019a and 2019b).

OLAF is also in charge of communicating its discoveries to the Union's bodies and institutions for follow-up and it is important to point out that authorizing officers are capable of actually excluding applicants who are not regarded as reliable from the Union's funding or flag suspicions (European Anti-Fraud Office, 2019; OLAF/Anti-fraud, 2018; Vasileiou, 2013a, 2014a, 2017b, 2017c, 2018b, 2018c, 2019a and 2019b).

In particular, they manage to do that according to a) the specific audit findings of the Union's bodies and institutions, b) the findings of OLAF investigations and c) reports on irregularities detected by member state organizations and authorities that in fact implement the Union's spending programs. It is not difficult to realize the momentousness of such actions (European Anti-Fraud Office, 2019; OLAF/Anti-fraud, 2018; Vasileiou, 2013a, 2014a, 2017b, 2017c, 2018b, 2018c, 2019a and 2019b).

At this point, it is necessary to emphatically highlight the truly multidimensional role of the EDES, in the context of which, flagged or excluded applicants are systematically listed (European Anti-Fraud Office, 2019; OLAF/Anti-fraud, 2018; Vasileiou, 2013a, 2014a, 2017b, 2017c, 2018b, 2018c, 2019a and 2019b).

EDES satisfactorily replaced the previous Central Exclusion Database and Early Warning System from January 1, 2016. EDES comprises two principal parts. The first is the "Early Detection", which in reality includes certain (tremendously significant) information on organizations, people and companies that are highly probable to become dangerous for the Union's financial interests via fraud phenomena (European Anti-Fraud Office, 2019; OLAF/Anti-fraud, 2018; Vasileiou, 2013a, 2014a, 2017b, 2017c, 2018b, 2018c, 2019a and 2019b).

The second part is the "Exclusion", which contains details of organizations, people and companies banned from EU direct funding for specific reasons (European Anti-Fraud Office, 2019; OLAF/Anti-fraud, 2018; Vasileiou, 2013a, 2014a, 2017b, 2017c, 2018b, 2018c, 2019a and 2019b).

These reasons may be a) the fact that they have seriously ruptured the terms of a previous Union's contract, b) that they are bankrupt and c) that they have actually been found guilty of corruption, fraud or miscellaneous equally important crimes, or of negative professional behavior (European Anti-Fraud Office, 2019; OLAF/Anti-fraud, 2018; Vasileiou, 2013a, 2014a, 2017b, 2017c, 2018b, 2018c, 2019a and 2019b).

Attention must also be paid to the fact that member states and entrusted entities indeed apply their own rules when taking decisions as regards the kind of action they must take if an entity is actually recorded as "excluded" in terms of EDES (European Anti-Fraud Office, 2019; OLAF/Anti-fraud, 2018).

We have to stress the fact that all authorizing officers in Union's bodies and institutions, as well as their staff are indeed in position to access EDES on a need-to-know basis and this is an indeed remarkable feature that can result in numerous advantages (European Anti-Fraud Office, 2019; OLAF/Antifraud, 2018; Vasileiou, 2013a, 2014a, 2017b, 2017c, 2018b, 2018c, 2019a and 2019b).

However, it is worth mentioning that read access to the exclusion branch only is available to member state entities and authorities responsible for the implementation of EU spending programs (European Anti-Fraud Office, 2019; OLAF/Antifraud, 2018; Vasileiou, 2013a, 2014a, 2017b, 2017c, 2018b, 2018c, 2019a and 2019b).

According to our hitherto conducted research, we remain convinced that both IMS and EDES perform an enormous variety of significant tasks towards a better economic future. What is important, though, is to mention a specific connection between them (European Anti-Fraud Office, 2019; OLAF/Antifraud, 2018; Vasileiou, 2013a, 2014a, 2017b, 2017c, 2018b, 2018c, 2019a and 2019b).

At least in our opinion, the objective is for EDES users in the Union's bodies and institutions to be capable of satisfactorily consult the particularly useful IMS data while considering an application for Union funding. We have to elucidate that IMS solely covers the so-called "shared management" activities, which are being managed by the Commission together with member states (European Anti-Fraud Office, 2019; OLAF/Anti-fraud, 2018).

Nonetheless, we must point out that entities which actually take part as either contractors or beneficiaries in the context of shared management actions may also apply for grants or contracts managed directly by the Commission or miscellaneous Union bodies (European Anti-Fraud Office, 2019; OLAF/Anti-fraud, 2018; Vasileiou, 2013a, 2014a, 2017b, 2017c, 2018b, 2018c, 2019a and 2019b).

Such a detail is of paramount noteworthiness due to the fact that in these cases, if the applying entity is flagged in IMS, the IMS record is capable of successfully be used so as to take a decision on the precise measures that they have to be taken in order for the Union's financial interests to be adequately safeguarded (European Anti-Fraud Office, 2019; OLAF/Anti-fraud, 2018; Vasileiou, 2013a, 2014a, 2017b, 2017c, 2018b, 2018c, 2019a and 2019b).

In the following (and final) chapter, the most important concluding remarks have been methodically summarized in the wider context of our attempts to satisfactorily justify our principal arguments. Our dominant objective has been to take all the relevant developments meticulously into account in order to come up with a number of thoughts concerning the near or the distant future. We believe that this book will have fully achieved its objectives if our concluding remarks provide the reader with impetus for even more fruitful future research.

CHAPTER 3

CONCLUDING REMARKS

Our hitherto conducted analysis leads us to the conclusion that taxation and fraud prevention can indeed be linked in more than a few cases. Numerous EU activities are directly or indirectly associated with the two aforesaid areas and it would not be an exaggeration to state that both taxation and anti-fraud policies determine a vast array of EU decisions on an enormous variety of crucial matters.

Our principal aim through this book has been to methodically combine taxation with anti-fraud policies and come up with a number of specific suggestions on how they can both be sufficiently improved in the future for the benefit of all EU citizens who do not perform illegal actions.

As expected, the economic crisis provided the Union with additional impetus in order to be capable of successfully carrying out an even more methodical planning of actions and policies with regard to both taxation and fraud prevention.

A fairer tax system, accompanied by an even more successful anti-corruption mechanism can incontrovertibly boost growth and development within the EU. Moreover, it is not difficult to realize that the importance of a highly functional taxation system can actually become evident not only in terms of the economic, but also of the social sphere. After all, economic growth and progress are highly probable to result in social stability and vice versa.

Apart from that, we are certain that the elimination of corruption within the Union will significantly revitalize the relationship of mutual trust between the EU and its citizens.

Within the taxation context, tremendously noteworthy components such as the ATAD 1&2, the CCCTB, the Digital Single Market, the Digital Services Tax, and the three pillars on which the Union's Agenda for the much-needed fair taxation is based have been emphatically highlighted due to their unquestionable magnitude.

What is more, in terms of the incessant and highly systematic anti-fraud battle, pivotal elements such as OLAF, the "Hercule Programmes", the IMS and the EDES have been rigorously examined. We decided not to enter into too many details which would probably perplex the reader, but opted for a more methodical and less complicated analysis in order to provide a coherent general framework without however omitting pivotal details.

We strongly believe that the success stories on which we have critically focused indubitably reveal OLAF's truly multidimensional character and it would be no exaggeration to argue that OLAF has so far performed colossal work. In these cases, numbers indeed tell the truth and we remain perfectly sure that in the future OLAF's role will be even more significant.

The economic crisis left more than a few wounds that the Union is systematically (and thus far sufficiently, at least in our opinion) attempting to heal. In order to witness more positive results a) there should be no dark points or loopholes as regards tax policy and b) all phenomena of fraud, corruption and other illegal practices must be eliminated as soon as possible.

Thus far, the cooperation between the Union and its member states has indubitably been satisfactory, but it is practically impossible to come up with accurate predictions regarding the distant future. Nonetheless, such a degree of cooperation is irrefutably positive and makes us optimistic that any serious future economic problems will be sufficiently addressed.

The crisis has taught the Union numerous important lessons, therefore, we remain certain that mistakes will not be repeated. What is more, this cooperation is a sign of deeper integration which has always been one of the dominant EU targets. A strong and united Europe can indisputably be characterized as a top-class global player directly influencing world politics.

Hence, in order for Europe to remain strong and for economic growth to be accompanied by social harmony, corruption signs are no longer permitted. Future challenges are highly probable to be far more complicated, but we are sure that the Union possesses both the will and the know-how so as to efficaciously address them.

BIBLIOGRAPHY

Bettendorf, Leon, Devereux, Michael P., van der Horst, Albert, Loretz, Simon, de Mooij, Ruud A., Jacobs, Bas and Wasmer, Etienne (2010), "Corporate tax harmonization in the EU [with Discussion]", *Economic Policy*, 25 (63), pp. 537-590.

Cipriani, Gabriele (2014), *Financing the EU Budget-Moving Forward or Backwards?* (London: Rowman & Littlefield International, Ltd.), available at https://www.ceps.eu/system/files/Financing%20 the%20EU%20budget_Final_Colour.pdf (accessed on 7/1/17).

Devereux, Michael P. and Loretz, Simon (2012), "How Would EU Corporate Tax Reform Affect US Investment in Europe?", *Tax Policy and the Economy*, 26 (1), pp. 59-92.

Europa/Budget (2017), "Budget" (in Greek), available at https://europa.eu/european-union/topics/budget_el (accessed on 4/1/17).

Europa/How the EU budget is spent (2017), "How the EU budget is spent" (in Greek), available at https://europa.eu/european-union/about-eu/money/expenditure_el (accessed on 4/2/17).

Europa/How the EU is funded (2017) "How the EU is funded" (in Greek), available at https://europa.eu/european-union/about-eu/money/revenue-income_el (accessed on 4/2/17).

Europa/Money and the EU (2017), "Money and the EU" (in Greek), available at https://europa.eu/european-union/about-eu/money_el (accessed on 4/2/17).

European Anti-Fraud Office (2019), "Home", available at https://ec.europa.eu/anti-fraud/ (accessed on 15/3/17).

European Commission (2018), "The euro", available at https://ec.europa.eu/info/business-economy-euro/ euro-area/euro_en (accessed on 14/7/18).

BIBLIOGRAPHY

European Commission/Budget (2014), "The European Union Explained-Budget" (in Greek), available at https://europa.eu/european-union/topics/budget_el (the document is included in this webpage) (accessed on 5/1/17).

European Commission/Taxation (2015), "The European Union Explained-Taxation" (in Greek), available at https://publications.europa.eu/el/publication-detail/-/publication/b075f231-bd9b-4e10-b4a3-7f248360c5ae (accessed on 21/7/18).

European Commission/Taxation (2018), "A Fair Share-Taxation in the EU for the 21st century", available at https://publications.europa.eu/en/publication-detail/-/publication/eba39edd-72a1-11e8-9483-01aa75ed71a1/language-en/format-PDF (accessed on 10/3/19).

European Union (2019), "Taxation", available at https://europa.eu/european-union/topics/taxation_en (accessed on 9/3/19).

European Union/Fraud (2018), "Fraud prevention" (in Greek), available at https://europa.eu/european-union/topics/fraud-prevention_el (accessed on 14/7/18).

European Union/Taxation (2018), "Taxation" (in Greek), available at https://europa.eu/european-union/topics/taxation_el (accessed on 20/7/18).

Janeba, Eckhart and Peters, Wolfgang (1999), "Tax Evasion, Tax Competition and the Gains from Nondiscrimination: The Case of Interest Taxation in Europe", *The Economic Journal*, 109 (452), pp. 93-101.

Keen, Michael, Smith, Stephen, Baldwin, Richard E. and Christiansen, Vidar (1996), "The Future of Value Added Tax in the European Union", *Economic Policy*, 11 (23), pp. 373-420.

BIBLIOGRAPHY

Lierse, Hanna (2012), "European taxation during the crisis: does politics matter?", *Journal of Public Policy*, 32 (3), pp. 207-230.

Matthijs, Herman (2010), "The Budget of the European Union", Institute for European Studies, available at http://www.ies.be/node/1062 (accessed on 7/2/17).

McKee, Martin and Gilmore, Anna B (2016), "European watchdog is failing to hold tobacco industry to account over smuggling", *BMJ: British Medical Journal*, 351.

Núñez Ferrer, Jorge (2007), "The EU Budget-The UK Rebate and the CAP-Phasing them both out?" CEPS Task Force Report (Brussels: Centre for European Policy Studies), available at http://aei.pitt.edu/9533/2/9533.pdf (accessed on 13/2/17).

OLAF (2017), "OLAF-European Anti-Fraud Office" (in Greek), available at http://ec.europa.eu/anti-fraud/home_el (accessed on 2/2/17).

OLAF (2018), "European Commission-European Anti-Fraud Office" (in Greek), available at https://ec.europa.eu/anti-fraud/home_el (accessed on 14/7/18).

OLAF/Anti-fraud (2018), "Anti-fraud policy", available at https://ec.europa.eu/anti-fraud/policy/preventing-fraud_en (accessed on 15/3/19).

OLAF/Figures (2018), "OLAF in figures", available at https://ec.europa.eu/anti-fraud/investigations/fraud-figures_en (accessed on 15/3/19).

OLAF/Fraud (2018), "Fraud prevention", available at https://europa.eu/european-union/topics/fraud-prevention_en (accessed on 13/3/19).

OLAF/History (2018), "History", available at https://ec.europa.eu/anti-fraud/about-us/history_en (accessed on 20/3/19).

BIBLIOGRAPHY

OLAF/Success stories (2018), "Success stories", available at https://ec.europa.eu/anti-fraud/investigations/success-stories_en (accessed on 15/3/19).

OLAF/What we do (2019), "What we do", available at https://ec.europa.eu/anti-fraud/about-us/mission_en (accessed on 20/3/19).

Radaelli, Claudio M. (1995), "Corporate Direct Taxation in the European Union: Explaining the Policy Process", *Journal of Public Policy,* 15 (2), pp. 153-181.

Turner, Clive (1995), "Smuggling Of Tobacco In Europe", *BMJ: British Medical Journal,* 311 (6999), p. 263.

Vasileiou, Ioannis (2013a), *European Unification-A Process of Convergence, or Divergence?* (in Greek) (Athens: Historical Quest).

Vasileiou, Ioannis (2013b), "1980-1999, European Union: The Years of Expansion and Enlargement", *From Hitler's New Europe to Merkel's Eurozone* (in Greek), Vol. 1, Historical Archive of Ependytis, pp. 76-95.

Vasileiou, Ioannis (2014a), *European Unification-A Process of Convergence, or Divergence?* (2nd Edition-Special Edition for Universities) (in Greek) (Athens: Historical Quest).

Vasileiou, Ioannis (2014b), *The Present and Future of the Agricultural Policy of the European Union* (in Greek) (Athens: Historical Quest).

Vasileiou, Ioannis (2015), *The Foreign and Security Policy of the European Union-A Critical Approach* (in Greek) (Athens: Historical Quest).

Vasileiou, Ioannis (2017a), *Climate Change: Manageable Problem or Slow Death of the Planet? EU Role and Actions until 2050-The Impact on Greece* (in Greek) (Athens: Historical Quest).

BIBLIOGRAPHY

Vasileiou, Ioannis (2017b), *Economic Crisis, Employment and Social Affairs in the European Union-Proposals and Actions to Combat Unemployment* (in Greek) (Athens: Historical Quest).

Vasileiou, Ioannis (2017c), *EU Budget-Issues About the Allocation and Redistribution of Resources in the EU* (in Greek) (Athens: Historical Quest).

Vasileiou, Ioannis (2017d), *European Union and Energy-The Route Towards 2050-Thoughts, Ideas and Conclusions* (in Greek) (Athens: Historical Quest).

Vasileiou, Ioannis (2017e), *The European Union Expansion Into Space* (in Greek) (Athens: Historical Quest).

Vasileiou, Ioannis (2018a), *Climate Change: Manageable Problem or Slow Death of the Planet? European Union Role and Actions until 2050-The Impact on Greece* (The Greek edition translated into English) (Independently Published-Available through Amazon).

Vasileiou, Ioannis (2018b), *Enterprises in the EU: Monopolies-Cartels-State Aid-Competition Rules* (in Greek) (Athens: Historical Quest).

Vasileiou, Ioannis (2018c), *European Union Budget-Issues About the Allocation and Redistribution of Resources in the European Union* (The Greek edition translated into English) (Independently Published-Available through Amazon).

Vasileiou, Ioannis (2018d), *The European Union Expansion Into Space* (The Greek edition translated into English) (Independently Published-Available through Amazon).

Vasileiou, Ioannis (2019a), *Economic Crisis, Employment and Social Affairs in the European Union-Proposals and Actions to Combat*

BIBLIOGRAPHY

Unemployment (The Greek edition translated into English) (Independently Published-Available through Amazon).

Vasileiou, Ioannis (2019b), *Enterprises in the EU-Monopolies-Cartels-State Aid-Competition Rules* (The Greek edition translated into English) (Independently Published-Available through Amazon).

Vasileiou, Ioannis (2019c), *European Union and Energy-The Route towards 2050-Thoughts, ideas and conclusions* (The Greek edition translated into English) (Independently Published-Available through Amazon).

Vasileiou, Ioannis (2019d), *The Foreign and Security Policy of the European Union: A Critical Approach* (2nd fully revised edition) (The first edition was published in Greek in 2015) (Independently Published-Available through Amazon).

IOANNIS VASILEIOU

BIOGRAPHY

Ioannis Vasileiou was born in Athens in 1978. In 2001, he was awarded his Ptychio (equivalent to Bachelor's degree) in Political Science and Public Administration from the University of Athens (Greece). In 2003, he was awarded his first Master's degree (International Political Economy) from the University of Warwick (UK). In 2005, he was awarded his second Master's degree (International Economic Management) from the University of Birmingham (UK). In 2011, he was awarded his PhD from the University of Birmingham (UK) with specialization in the economic and political aspects of the European Union's Regional Policy. Since 2011, he has been conducting academic research on issues related to the European Union and international politics and economics.

www.ingramcontent.com/pod-product-compliance
Lightning Source LLC
Chambersburg PA
CBHW072206170526
45158CB00004BB/1777